Home and Back with Books

Written by Kimberly Jordano

Illustrator: Pattie Silver-Thompson

Editor: Joel Kupperstein

Project Director: Carolea Williams

CTP ©1996, Creative Teaching Press, Inc., Cypress, CA 90630

Table of Contents

Introduction

Home and Back with Books provides fun, motivating take-home activity kits that connect children's experiences at school with their daily lives at home. Each kit invites children and their families to read a literature selection and complete related activities using hands-on manipulatives and journal recording pages.

Activities are organized into three sections—Math, Science, and Just-for-Fun—and presented in pairs. Each pair of activity kits includes one page of assembly directions (half-page per kit), followed by the reproducibles needed for those kits. Here is an example of a typical take-home kit.

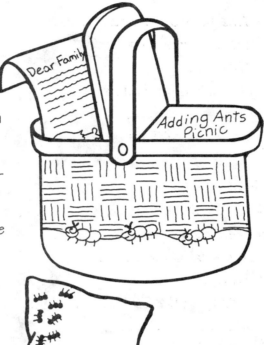

Family Letters

Family letters provide activity introductions and easy-to-follow instructions. To make a letter more functional and durable, attach it to a sheet of construction paper, add a class list to the back, and laminate the paper. Use class lists to track which students have taken activities home.

Reproducibles

Many kits include corresponding reproducibles, often in the form of journal activities. Include a completed sample with each kit. Bind blank pages behind the sample in a folder or binder, and have students complete a page in a pre-assembled class journal.

Manipulatives

Manipulatives such as plastic bugs, magnetic letters, buttons, seeds, and magazine cutouts are recommended with many activity kits. Children use these manipulatives in hands-on sorting, counting, patterning, writing, and science activities.

Emergent Readers

Each kit features a title from the *Learn to Read* series of emergent readers published by Creative Teaching Press. While the *Learn to Read* books are excellent complements to the kits, the activities can be completed using other literature titles as well. Send home more than one selection with each activity to give students a choice and an opportunity for more reading.

Management Tips

- Start slowly. Send home only one or two activities each day until you and your students get used to them. Circulate activities until all students have taken them home.

- Ask families for old canvas tote bags, plastic canisters, burlap sacks, or any other useful container. Invite them to sew labels and decorations on containers.

- Have a "work day" when parent volunteers can come to school and help prepare materials and containers.

- Write the name of each activity on its container in marker or paint.

- Enclose loose materials in plastic bags to prevent them from getting lost.

- To prevent family letters from being lost, attach them to their containers with yarn or twine,

- Prepare materials in advance. For example, if each child needs a bag of soil to complete an activity, have all bags ready so you won't need to fill one each time you send the kit home.

- Send home paperback books with kits whenever possible. Paperbacks are less expensive to replace if lost.

- Display the contents of a kit and demonstrate the activity before sending the kit home for the first time.

- Be sure students know how many of each manipulative are in the kits and how many they are expected to return.

- Designate an area for the checkout and return of take-home activities. Store containers on shelves or coat racks. Be sure students check off their names on the class list attached to each kit.

In working with the kits, family members may read stories to their children or listen as children read to them. After reading, family members help their children complete hands-on activities that complement the literature. Activities can be easily completed in one evening and returned to school the following day.

As you incorporate take-home activities into your curriculum, students become more motivated to read, enthusiastic about homework, excited about their families' involvement, and eager to handle greater responsibilities. Students' added enthusiasm for reading, coupled with extra opportunities to read, will naturally make them better readers.

Adding Ants Picnic

What's Inside . . .

- *Little Number Stories: Addition*
- family letter (page 6)
- journal (page 7)
- 25–30 plastic or paper ants, or black beans
- pencil/crayons

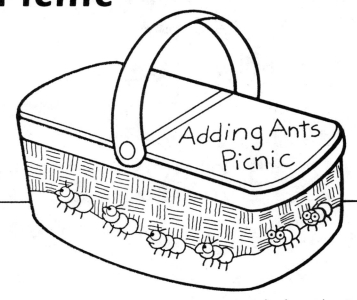

picnic basket with painted ants

More Take-Home Titles

Amazing Anthony Ant by Lorna and Graham Philpot (Random House)

Miss Spider's Tea Party by David Kirk (Callaway Editions)

Bug Bucket

What's Inside . . .

- *The Bugs Go Marching*
- family letter (page 8)
- 60 plastic or paper bugs (page 9)

plastic bucket with painted bugs and bug stickers

More Take-Home Titles

Amazing Anthony Ant by Lorna and Graham Philpot (Random House)

How Many Bugs in a Box? by David A. Carter (Simon & Schuster)

Spiders, Spiders Everywhere! (Creative Teaching Press)

Math

Adding Ants Picnic

Dear Family,

In math we have been working on our addition skills. Tonight your child brought home a special addition book and activity. Enjoy working together as you complete the following steps:

1. Read the addition story.

2. Use the ants in the container to act out the story, adding as you go.

3. Make up your own addition story with the ants. Write and illustrate the number sentence in the Adding Ants Picnic Journal.

Be sure to put the ants back in the container and return the activity to school tomorrow!

Thank you!

Home and Back with Books © 1996 Creative Teaching Press

Adding Ants Picnic Journal

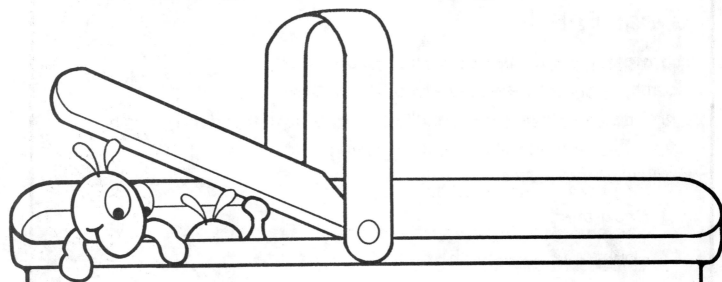

_____ ants are having lunch. _____ more join them.

Now there are _____ ants at the picnic!

_____ + _____ = _____

Draw a picture of your ants equation and the foods they ate.

Bug Bucket

Dear Family,

In math we have been working on counting, patterning, and sorting skills. Tonight your child brought home the Bug Bucket to share with you. Please help him or her complete the following activities:

1. Read the bug book.

2. Count the bugs in the bucket. Try counting them by fives and tens.

3. Try sorting the bugs by size, color, and type of bug.

4. Make a pattern with your bugs. Pattern them by size, color, or type of bug.

Recount the bugs to make sure you have them all. Place the bugs in the bucket and return it to school tomorrow.

Thank you!

Home and Back with Books © 1996 Creative Teaching Press

Paper Bugs

Math

Button Bag

What's Inside . . .

- *Buttons Buttons*
- family letter (page 11)
- bag of buttons
- plastic sorting tray

patterning

canvas tote bag with buttons sewn on

More Take-Home Titles

Big Bear and the Blue Button by Stephanie Laslett (Derry Dale)
The Button Box by Margaret Reid (Dutton)

Crayon Count Backpack

What's Inside . . .

- *The Crayola® Counting Book*
- family letter (page 12)
- Crayon Class Book (page 13)
- small, medium, and large packs of crayons

backpack decorated with painted crayons

More Take-Home Titles

A-Counting We Will Go (Creative Teaching Press)
Fish Eyes by Lois Ehlert (Harcourt Brace Jovanovich)
One Gorilla by Atsuko Morozumi (Farrar, Straus)

Button Bag

Dear Family,

We have been learning about sorting in math. Tonight your child brought home the Button Bag to practice sorting. Enjoy the enclosed book and have fun completing the activities!

1. Read the sorting book together.

2. Sort the buttons in the sorting tray. Try sorting them by attributes such as color, size, shape, and number of holes.

3. Play "Guess My Sorting Rule." Have one person sort buttons, keeping the attribute a secret, while other players guess the sorting rule.

Happy sorting! Please return the Button Bag tomorrow.

Math

Crayon Count Backpack

Dear Family,

Tonight your child brought home the Crayon Count Backpack. In math we have been learning about counting and patterning. Please help your child complete the following activities:

1. Read the counting book.

2. Count the crayons in the small pack, the medium-sized pack, and the large pack.

3. How many red crayons can you find? blue? yellow? green?

4. Make a pattern with your crayons, such as **red, blue, green; red, blue, green.**

5. Draw a picture in the Crayon Class Book.

Happy counting, and please return the backpack tomorrow for another student to enjoy!

Home and Back with Books © 1996 Creative Teaching Press

Crayon Class Book

_____'s Crayon Creation
(your name)

I drew a _____ with my crayons.

Math

Dinosaur Counting Carrier

What's Inside . . .

- *The Skip Count Song*
- family letter (page 15)
- journal (page 16)
- rubber dinosaur stamps
- stamp pads
- pencil/crayons

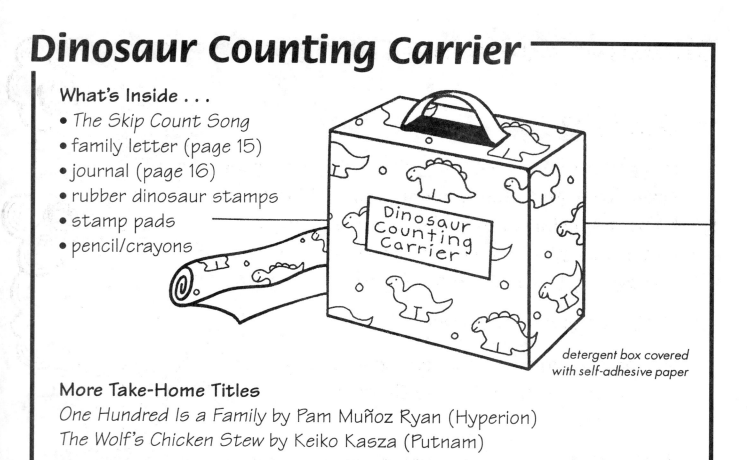

detergent box covered
with self-adhesive paper

More Take-Home Titles

One Hundred Is a Family by Pam Muñoz Ryan (Hyperion)

The Wolf's Chicken Stew by Keiko Kasza (Putnam)

Fraction Fun Pack

What's Inside . . .

- *Lunch with Cat and Dog*
- family letter (page 17)
- play dough
- craft stick
- plastic work mat

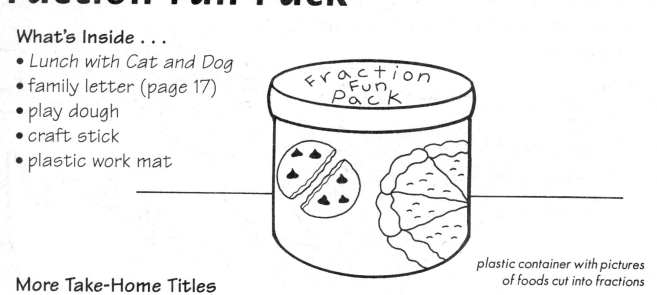

plastic container with pictures
of foods cut into fractions

More Take-Home Titles

The Doorbell Rang by Pat Hutchins (Scholastic)

Eating Fractions by Bruce McMillan (Scholastic)

The Little Mouse, the Red Ripe Strawberry, and the Big Hungry Bear
   by Don and Audrey Wood (Scholastic)

Dinosaur Counting Carrier

Dear Family,

In math we have been learning to count by ones, twos, fives, and tens. Tonight your child brought home a special counting book and activity to share with you. Enjoy sharing the book and completing the activity together!

1. Read the counting book.

2. Use the dinosaur stamps to stamp groups of two, five, or ten in the Dinosaur Counting Journal.

3. Practice counting by twos, fives, and tens to 100.

Have fun counting, stamping, and recording! Please return the Dinosaur Counting Carrier tomorrow.

Math

Dinosaur Counting Journal

Stamp dinosaurs to show how you counted.

_____ can count by _____.
(your name)   (twos, fives, or tens)

Home and Back with Books © 1996 Creative Teaching Press

Fraction Fun Pack

Dear Family,

In math we have been learning about fractions. Tonight your child brought home a special fraction book and activity to share with you. Please help him or her with the following steps:

1. Read the fraction story. Notice how foods are cut into various fractions.

2. As you reread the book, work with play dough on the work mat to make different "foods." Use the craft stick to cut the foods in halves, thirds, and fourths.

3. Think of other foods you can make and cut into equal parts to share with your family.

Have fun, and be sure to return the Fraction Fun Pack to school tomorrow!

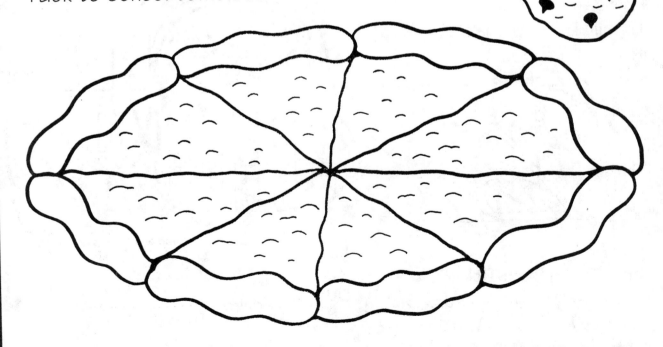

Math

Giant Cookie Jar

What's Inside . . .
- *Who Took the Cookies from the Cookie Jar?*
- family letter (page 19)
- 10–15 plastic or paper cookies

plastic jar with painted cookies

More Take-Home Titles
Little Number Stories: Subtraction (Creative Teaching Press)
Roll Over by Merle Peek (Clarion)
There Were Ten in the Bed by Pam Adams (Child's Play)

Graphing Bag

What's Inside . . .
- *We Can Make Graphs*
- family letter (page 20)
- journal (page 21)
- pencil/crayons

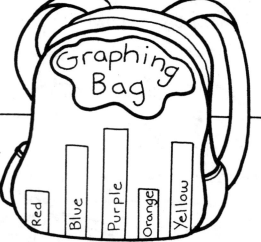

backpack decorated with colors and graphs

More Take-Home Titles
A Three-Hat Day by Laura Geringer (HarperCollins)
Shoes by Elizabeth Winthrop (HarperTrophy)

Giant Cookie Jar

Dear Family,

In math we have been working on subtraction skills. Your child has brought home a special subtraction book and activity to share with you. Please help him or her complete the following steps:

1. Read the subtraction story.

2. Count to make sure you have at least ten cookies in the jar.

3. Reread the story and subtract cookies from the jar as you read. Each time you subtract cookies, count to see how many are left in the jar. (If you wish, write subtraction sentences on scratch paper.)

4. Make up your own subtraction stories using the cookies in the jar.

Have a yummy time subtracting! Place the cookies and book in the container and return it to school tomorrow.

Home and Back with Books © 1996 Creative Teaching Press

Math

Graphing Bag

Dear Family,

Tonight your child brought home a special graphing book and activity. In math we have been working on our graphing skills. Please help your child complete the following steps:

1. Read the book together.

2. Take a survey of your friends' and family's favorite colors.

3. Complete a page of the Color Graphing Journal.

4. Talk about three things you learned from your graph.

Have fun, and be sure to return the Graphing Bag to school tomorrow!

Thank you!

Home and Back with Books © 1996 Creative Teaching Press

Color Graphing Journal

_____'s Friends' and Family's Favorite Colors
(your name)

	Red	Orange	Yellow	Blue	Green	Purple	Brown	Pink
9								
8								
7								
6								
5								
4								
3								
2								
1								

Math

Great Pumpkin Pail

What's Inside . . .
- *Our Pumpkin*
- family letter (page 23)
- string
- pumpkin seeds or dried lima beans
- small food scale
- 10 small cups

plastic pumpkin pail with handle

More Take-Home Titles

The Biggest Pumpkin Ever by Steven Kroll (Scholastic)

Mousekin's Golden House by Edna Miller (Simon & Schuster)

I Can Tell Time Tote

What's Inside . . .
- *What Time Is It?*
- family letter (page 24)
- journal (page 25)
- play clock
- pencil/crayons

canvas tote bag with painted clock

More Take-Home Titles

Big Time Bears by Stephen Krensky (Little, Brown)

The Completed Hickory Dickory Dock by Jim Aylesworth (Macmillan)

The Grouchy Ladybug by Eric Carle (HarperCollins)

Great Pumpkin Pail

Dear Family,

In math we have been exploring measurement. Tonight your child brought home a book about pumpkins to practice measuring. Enjoy working together to complete the following activities:

1. Read the pumpkin story.

2. Estimate the distance around the pail, and cut a piece of string the length of your guess.

3. Use your string to measure the distance around the pail. Was your guess too long, too short, or just right?

4. Weigh the pail twice—once with the seeds inside and once without.

5. Will the pail float? Place it in a bathtub or sink filled with water and find out.

6. Count the seeds. Use the cups to count by tens.

Have fun, and please return the Great Pumpkin Pail tomorrow!

Math

I Can Tell Time Tote

Dear Family,

Tonight your child brought home the I Can Tell Time Tote. In math we have been learning to tell time to the hour and would like to practice with you at home. Enclosed, you will find a play clock, time book, and Time Journal. Work together to complete the following steps:

1. Read the time book together.

2. Reread the story, moving the hands on the play clock to match the book.

3. Practice telling time by naming a time of day and showing it on the clock. Tell something you might do at each time of day. For a challenge, show times to the half hour.

4. Think of your favorite time of day and illustrate it in the Time Journal.

Have fun, and be sure to return the I Can Tell Time Tote tomorrow for another student to enjoy!

Time Journal

_____'s favorite time of day is _____ o'clock
(your name)

because _____

_____

_____.

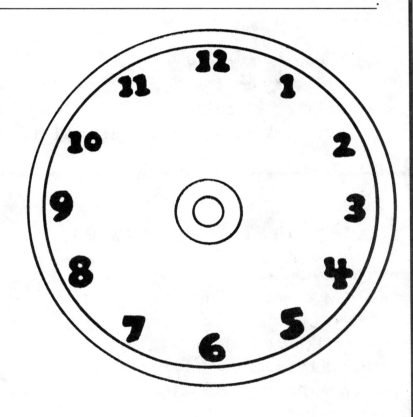

Math

Let's Measure It Box

What's Inside . . .
- *Let's Measure It!*
- family letter (page 27)
- journal (page 28)
- measuring tools (ruler, tape measure, string, plastic snap cubes)
- pencil/crayons

plastic box covered with ruler and number stickers

More Take-Home Titles
Inch by Inch by Leo Lionni (Astor-Honor)
Jim and the Beanstalk by Raymond Briggs (Sandcastle)
Ten Beads Tall by Pam Adams (Child's Play)

Magic Money Bag

What's Inside . . .
- *The Magic Money Box*
- family letter (page 29)
- journal (page 30)
- magician's cape
- magic wand (glitter-covered wooden dowel)
- Magic Money Box (decorated shoe box)
- play money
- rubber money stamps
- stamp pads
- pencil/crayons

drawstring bag decorated with "magic" designs

More Take-Home Titles
Alexander, Who Used to Be Rich Last Sunday by Judith Viorst (Macmillan)
26 Letters and 99 Cents by Tana Hoban (Greenwillow)

Let's Measure It Box

Dear Family,

In math we have been learning about measurement. Tonight your child brought home the Let's Measure It Box and a book to share with you. Please help him or her complete the following activities:

1. Read the measuring book.

2. Practice measuring items in your home using string, snap cubes, and other tools in the box. Measure items longer than, shorter than, and equal to the tools you use.

3. Illustrate one item you measured in the Measuring Journal.

Be sure to return the Let's Measure It Box tomorrow so another student can take it home to share.

Thank you!

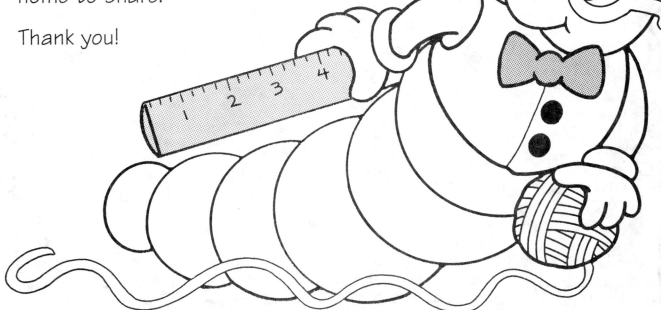

Math

Measuring Journal

_____ measured _____.
(your name)

It was _____ _____ long.
(measurement unit)

Here is a picture of what I measured.

Home and Back with Books © 1996 Creative Teaching Press

Magic Money Bag

Dear Family,

We have been learning the names and values of coins in math. Tonight your child brought home the Magic Money Bag. Inside, you will find a money book and materials for practicing money skills. Enjoy working together as you complete the following activities:

1. Read the money book. Count the coins on each page.

2. Reread the story, placing corresponding real money on the pages and naming each coin as you go.

3. Put on the cape and do your own "money magic." For example, place coins in the box, wave the wand and say, **Abracadabra, I will find a dime in the Magic Money Box!** Open the box and find the correct coin. Try to perform a magic trick for each coin.

4. Collect all coins when you are done, and place them inside the box.

5. Complete a page in the Magic Money Journal.

Enjoy, and please return the Magic Money Bag to school tomorrow!

Math

Magic Money Journal

With my magic wand, I can turn _____
(number and name of coin)

into _____.
(number and name of coin)

Here is a picture.

Home and Back with Books © 1996 Creative Teaching Press

Number Writing Box

What's Inside . . .

- *A-Counting We Will Go*
- family letter (page 32)
- laminated sentence strips
  with number patterns
  such as 1, 2, 1, 2, 1 . . .
- blank, laminated sentence
  strips for student practice
- erasable markers

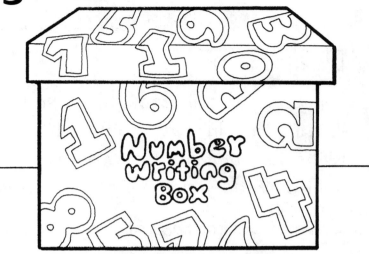

box covered with self-adhesive paper and number stickers

More Take-Home Titles

Mouse Count by Ellen Stoll Walsh (Harcourt Brace Jovanovich)

One Bear at Bedtime by Mick Inkpen (Little, Brown)

Seven Eggs by Meredith Hooper (HarperCollins)

Pattern Hunting Pack

What's Inside . . .

- *I See Patterns*
- family letter (page 33)
- journal (page 34)
- rubber stamps
  (various designs)
- stamp pads (two colors)
- pencil/crayons

shoe box decorated with sticker patterns

More Take-Home Titles

Drummer Hoff by Barbara Emberley (Simon & Schuster)

My Mom and Dad Make Me Laugh by Nick Sharrat (Candlewick)

Math

Number Writing Box

Dear Family,

Tonight your child brought home the Number Writing Box. In math we have been learning to write our numbers. Enjoy reading and working with your child as you complete the following activities:

1. Read the number story.

2. Using an erasable marker, trace over the number pattern and continue it to the end of the strip.

3. Wipe the strip clean with a damp towel and begin a new one. Write your own pattern on a blank pattern strip.

Happy writing! Be sure to put all items in the box and return it to school tomorrow so another friend can practice writing numbers.

Home and Back with Books © 1996 Creative Teaching Press

Pattern Hunting Pack

Dear Family,

In math we have been learning about patterns. Tonight your child brought home a special pattern book and activity. Please help him or her complete the following steps:

1. Read the pattern book.

2. Go on a "pattern hunt" in your home. Look for patterns in clothing, toys, dishes, towels, and other places.

3. Complete a page in the Pattern Hunting Journal using stamps and stamp pads. Be sure to label your pattern (e.g., **big, little, big, little; red, blue, red, blue; A, B, A, B**).

Happy patterning, and please return the Pattern Hunting Pack tomorrow!

Math

Pattern Hunting Journal

All About _____'s Pattern

(your name)

I made a(n) _____ pattern.

Home and Back with Books © 1996 Creative Teaching Press

Pattern Pouch

What's Inside . . .
- *Mr. Noisy's Book of Patterns*
- family letter (page 36)
- journal (page 37)
- plastic snap cubes
- pencil/crayons

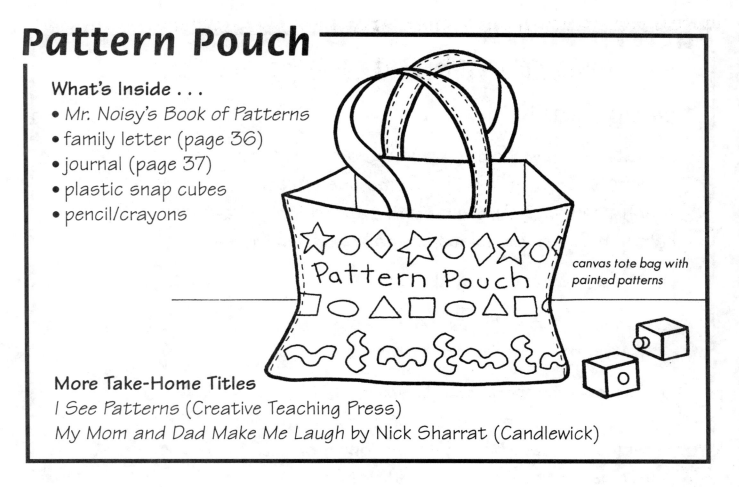

canvas tote bag with painted patterns

More Take-Home Titles
I See Patterns (Creative Teaching Press)
My Mom and Dad Make Me Laugh by Nick Sharrat (Candlewick)

Pizza Box

What's Inside . . .
- *Lunch with Cat and Dog*
- family letter (page 38)
- journal (page 39)
- Pizza Toppings (page 40)
- pencil/crayons

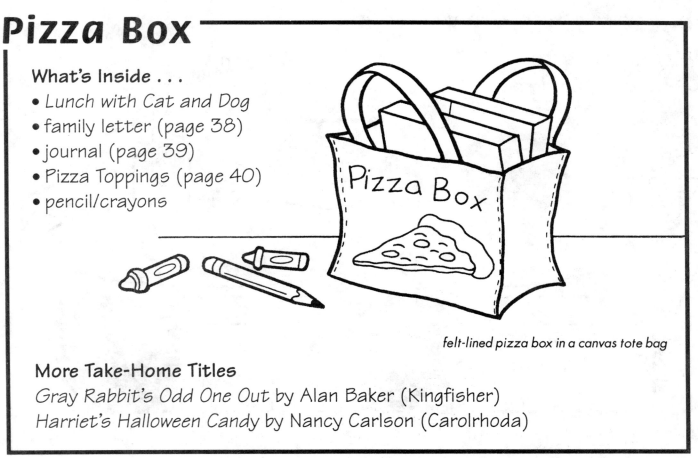

felt-lined pizza box in a canvas tote bag

More Take-Home Titles
Gray Rabbit's Odd One Out by Alan Baker (Kingfisher)
Harriet's Halloween Candy by Nancy Carlson (Carolrhoda)

Pattern Pouch

Dear Family,

In math we have been learning about patterns. Tonight your child brought home the Pattern Pouch to practice reading and patterning. Please help him or her complete the following activities:

1. Read the pattern book.

2. Connect the snap cubes in patterns that match patterns in the story.

3. Design a pattern and illustrate it in the Pattern Journal. For example, your pattern might be **tree, flower, tree, flower,** or **red stripe, green stripe, red stripe, green stripe.** See how creative you can be!

Happy patterning! Please return the Pattern Pouch tomorrow.

Pattern Journal

_____ made a pattern of _____ .
(your name)

Math

Pizza Box

Dear Family,

In math we have been learning about sorting. Tonight your child brought home a special sorting book and activity. Enjoy reading together, and have fun completing the following steps:

1. Read the sorting book.

2. Group the felt food in the pizza box by food type.

3. What other ways can you sort the food— by color, size, or any other way?

4. Design your favorite kind of pizza and illustrate it in the Pizza Journal.

Have a good time sorting, and please return the Pizza Box tomorrow!

Pizza Journal

Chef _____'s Pizza

(your name)

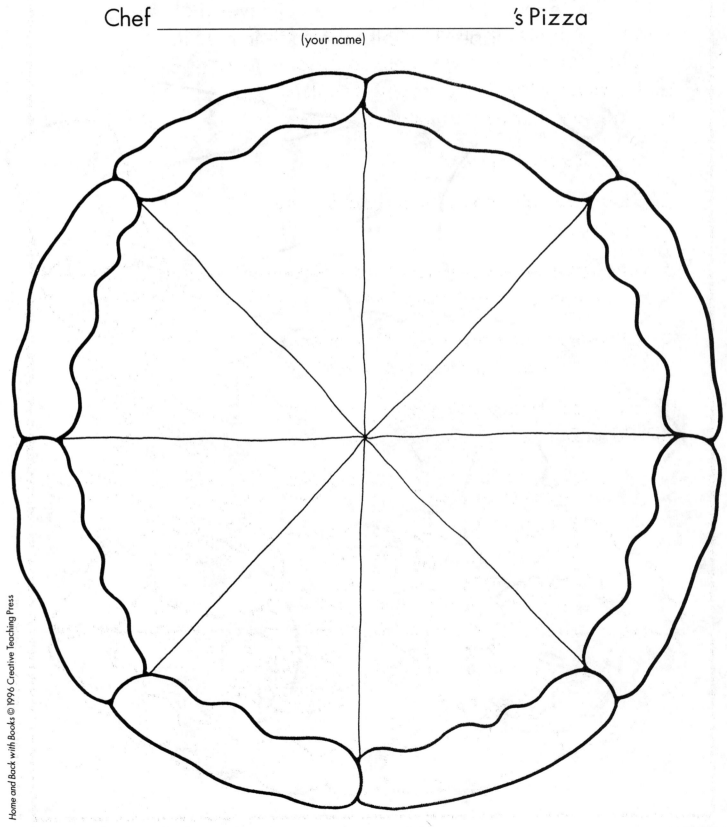

Math

Pizza Toppings

Teacher Note: In advance, cut several of each shape from felt to include in the kit.

Play Dough Counting Pack

What's Inside . . .
- *How Many?*
- family letter (page 42)
- laminated number cards
- play dough
- small cookie cutters
- plastic work mat

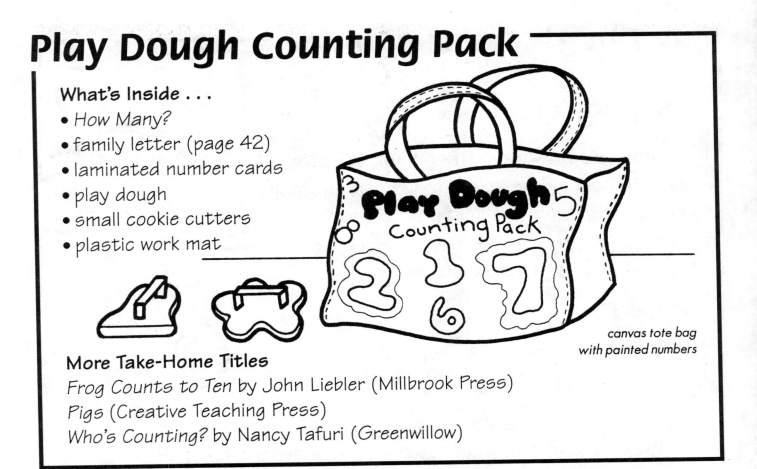

canvas tote bag with painted numbers

More Take-Home Titles

Frog Counts to Ten by John Liebler (Millbrook Press)

Pigs (Creative Teaching Press)

Who's Counting? by Nancy Tafuri (Greenwillow)

Shape Suitcase

What's Inside . . .
- *I See Shapes*
- family letter (page 43)
- journal (page 44)
- Paper Shapes (page 45)
- shape blocks (optional)
- scissors
- glue
- pencil/crayons

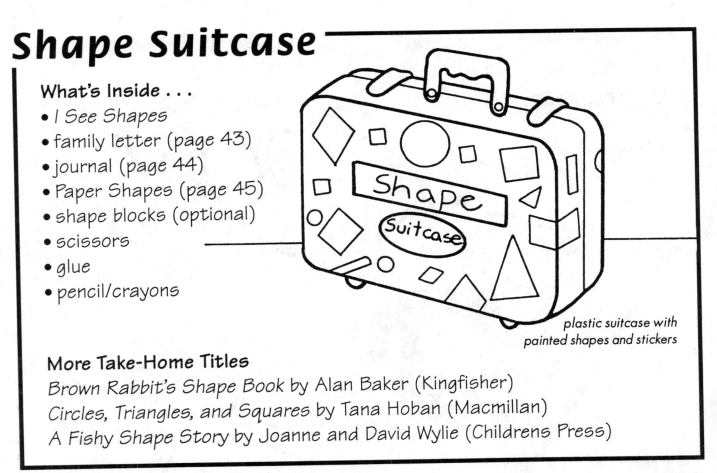

plastic suitcase with painted shapes and stickers

More Take-Home Titles

Brown Rabbit's Shape Book by Alan Baker (Kingfisher)

Circles, Triangles, and Squares by Tana Hoban (Macmillan)

A Fishy Shape Story by Joanne and David Wylie (Childrens Press)

Play Dough Counting Pack

Dear Family,

In math we have been working on counting and number recognition. Tonight your child brought home a special number book and activity. Enjoy working together as you complete the following steps:

1. Read the number book.

2. Use play dough to form numbers on the number cards.

3. Use the cookie cutters to make the correct number of play dough "cookies" to go with your number cards.

Have a great time counting, and please return the Play Dough Counting Pack tomorrow for another student to enjoy!

Home and Back with Books © 1996 Creative Teaching Press

Shape Suitcase

Dear Family,

In math we have been learning about shapes. Tonight your child brought home a shape book and activity. Please work with him or her to complete the following steps:

1. Read the shape book together.

2. Name each shape in the suitcase. Find different ways to sort them. For example, sort by size, color, or number of sides.

3. Use the shapes to make your own shape creation.

4. Show your shape creation by gluing paper shapes on a page of the Shape Journal.

Have fun, and please return the Shape Suitcase tomorrow!

Math

Shape Journal

_____'s Shape Creation
(your name)

I used these shapes:

▲ _____   ▬ _____   ■ _____

● _____   ⬭ _____   ◆ _____

Home and Back with Books © 1996 Creative Teaching Press

Paper Shapes

Teacher Note: In advance, prepare several of each
shape in different colors to include in the kit.
Each student will need a new set of shapes.

Math

Shark Bites Bag

What's Inside . . .
- *Little Number Stories: Subtraction*
- family letter (page 47)
- shark puppet
- dice
- 20 fish-shaped crackers in a plastic bag
- paper
- pencil

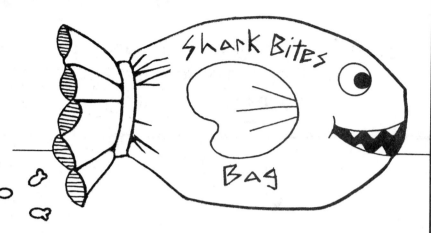

cloth bag decorated to look like a fish

More Take-Home Titles
Five Little Monkeys Jumping on the Bed by Eileen Christelow (Houghton Mifflin)

The Right Number of Elephants by Jeff Sheppard (HarperCollins)

Spider Sack

What's Inside . . .
- *Spiders, Spiders Everywhere!*
- family letter (page 48)
- journal (page 49)
- Spider Counting Mat (page 50)
- 60 plastic or paper spiders
- pencil/crayons

black drawstring sack made of loosely-tied cords

More Take-Home Titles
Miss Spider's Tea Party by David Kirk (Callaway Editions)

The Roly Poly Spider by Jill Sardegna (Scholastic)

The Very Busy Spider by Eric Carle (Philomel)

Shark Bites Bag

Dear Family,

In math we have been learning about subtraction. Tonight your child brought home the Shark Bites Bag and a special subtraction book to share with you. Please help him or her complete the following activities:

1. Read the subtraction story.

2. Using the shark puppet, fish-shaped crackers, and dice, play "Shark Attack."

How to Play Shark Attack

- Place fish crackers between you and your partner.
- Count ten crackers for each player.
- Take turns rolling a die and have the shark puppet "eat" the number of crackers shown on the die. (You may eat the crackers.)
- Write the subtraction sentence on scratch paper. For example, $10 - 2 = 8$.
  If the number on the die is greater than the number of crackers left, roll again.
- The first player to eat all ten crackers wins!

Watch out for sharks, and have a swimming good time! Please return the Shark Bites Bag tomorrow.

Math

Spider Sack

Dear Family,

Tonight your child brought home the Spider Sack to share with you. In math we are working on sorting, patterning, and counting. The Spider Sack contains a book and activities for you to share and complete together.

1. Read the spider story.

2. Count the spiders to make sure you have 60. Try counting by tens.

3. Place the correct number of spiders on each section of the counting mat.

4. Try sorting the spiders by size, color, and type.

5. Draw a spider on the Spider Journal.

6. Draw a pattern design on your spider.

Have a creepy-crawly good time, and please return the Spider Sack tomorrow!

Spider Journal

_____'s Spider Creation
(your name)

My spider has a(n) _____ pattern on its body.

Math

Spider Counting Mat

1 spider in a tree.

2 spiders chasing me.

3 spiders on the floor.

4 spiders crawling under the door.

5 spiders smile at me.

6 spiders say, "Whoopee!"

WHOOPEE!

7 spiders under the bed.

8 spiders on my head.

9 spiders on the wall.

1, 2, 3, 4...

10 spiders—count them all!

Time Tote

What's Inside . . .
- *The Time Song*
- family letter (page 52)
- stopwatch

canvas tote bag with painted stopwatch

More Take-Home Titles

Bear Child's Book of Hours by Anne Rockwell (HarperCollins)

Clocks and More Clocks by Pat Hutchins (Macmillan)

Time To . . . by Bruce McMillan (Lothrop)

What Comes in Twos? Tote

What's Inside . . .
- *What Comes in Threes?*
- family letter (page 53)
- journal (page 54)
- pencil/crayons

canvas tote bag decorated with painted objects

More Take-Home Titles

One Hundred Is a Family by Pam Muñoz Ryan (Hyperion)

The Skip Count Song (Creative Teaching Press)

What Comes in 2s, 3s, and 4s? by Suzanne Aker (Simon & Schuster)

Time Tote

Dear Family,

In math we have been measuring how long it takes to do different things. Tonight your child brought home the Time Tote. Please help him or her complete the following activities:

1. Read the time story.

2. Discuss how long it takes to make your bed, eat breakfast, brush your teeth, or take a bath.

3. Use the stopwatch to see how many times you can do the following tasks in one minute:
   - blink your eyes
   - clap your hands
   - jump
   - touch your toes
   - say your ABCs
   - bounce a ball

4. Find some other daily activities to time.

Have fun, and be sure to return the Time Tote tomorrow!

Home and Back with Books © 1996 Creative Teaching Press

What Comes in Twos? Tote

Dear Family,

In math we have been working on counting skills. Tonight your child brought home a special book and counting activity. Please help him or her complete the following steps:

1. Read the number book.

2. Name some objects that come in twos.

3. Complete a page in the What Comes in Twos? Journal.

Have fun finding groups of two! Please return the tote to school tomorrow.

shoes

socks

gloves

skates

Math

What Comes in Twos? Journal

_____ come in twos.

_____ come in twos.

_____ come in twos.

_____ come in twos.

But there is only one _____.
(your name)

Here is a picture.

Home and Back with Books © 1996 Creative Teaching Press

Farm Fannypack

What's Inside . . .
- *Down on the Farm*
- family letter (page 56)
- journal (page 57)
- plastic farm animals
- small, wooden building blocks
- pencil/crayons

large fannypack with painted farm animals

More Take-Home Titles
Barn Dance! by Bill Martin, Jr. and John Archambault (Holt)
Big Red Barn by Margaret Wise Brown (HarperCollins)
When the Rooster Crowed by Patricia Lillie (Greenwillow)

Forest Fun Pack

What's Inside . . .
- *Whose Forest Is It?*
- family letter (page 58)
- Forest Figures (page 59)
- scissors
- paper bag
- glue
- crayons

detergent box covered with self-adhesive paper and forest animal stickers

More Take-Home Titles
A Fairy Went A-Marketing by Rose Fyleman (Dutton)
We're Going on a Bear Hunt by Michael Rosen (Macmillan)
What the Moon Saw by Brian Wildsmith (Oxford)

Science

Farm Fannypack

Dear Family,

In science we have been learning about life on a farm. Tonight your child has brought home a special book to share with you. Enjoy reading the book with your child. Then, have fun creating a farm together.

1. Read the farm story.

2. Use the farm animals and building blocks to set up and play with your own farm.

3. Complete a page in the Down on the Farm Journal. Draw animals you might see on a farm.

Happy farming, and please return the Farm Fannypack tomorrow!

Down on the Farm Journal

The _____ on the farm says,

" _____, _____, _____."

Science

Forest Fun Pack

Dear Family,

In science we have been studying animal habitats. The forest is home to many animals. We are learning how important it is to keep the forest safe and clean. Enjoy sharing the forest book and creating a forest scene of your own.

1. Read the forest story.

2. Try to name all the animals in the story. What other forest animals can you name? What are some ways you can take care of the forest?

3. Color and cut out the forest figures and background. Glue the background to the paper bag and act out your own story, telling how you can take care of the forest. Store your animals in the paper bag when you are finished. You may keep your forest and animals!

Please return the Forest Fun Pack tomorrow for another Forest Ranger to enjoy!

Home and Back with Books © 1996 Creative Teaching Press

Forest Figures

Color and cut out the forest figures.
Glue the background to the paper bag.

Science

Habitat Handbag

What's Inside . . .
- *Who Lives Here?*
- family letter (page 61)
- journal (page 62)
- pencil/crayons

canvas tote bag with painted habitats

More Take-Home Titles

A House Is a House for Me by Mary Ann Hoberman (Viking)

Naptime, Laptime by Eileen Spinelli (Scholastic)

Who's Hiding? (Creative Teaching Press)

Is It Alive? Knapsack

What's Inside . . .
- *Is It Alive?*
- family letter (page 63)
- journal (page 64)
- nature pictures
- magnifying glass
- pencil/crayons

backpack decorated with a magnifying glass, rocks, and flowers

More Take-Home Titles

Animal, Vegetable, or Mineral? by Tana Hoban (Greenwillow)

Big Ones, Little Ones by Tana Hoban (Greenwillow)

Everything Grows by Raffi (Crown)

Habitat Handbag

Dear Family,

In science we have been studying animal habitats. Animals live in habitats that provide them with what they need to survive. Enjoy reading the enclosed book about animal homes and completing the following activities together.

1. Read the habitat book. Discuss why habitats in the book are good for the animals that live in them.

2. What animal habitats can you think of that were not discussed in the book?

3. Think of your favorite wild animal and complete a page of the Habitat Journal.

Have fun, and please return the Habitat Handbag tomorrow for someone else to enjoy!

Science

Habitat Journal

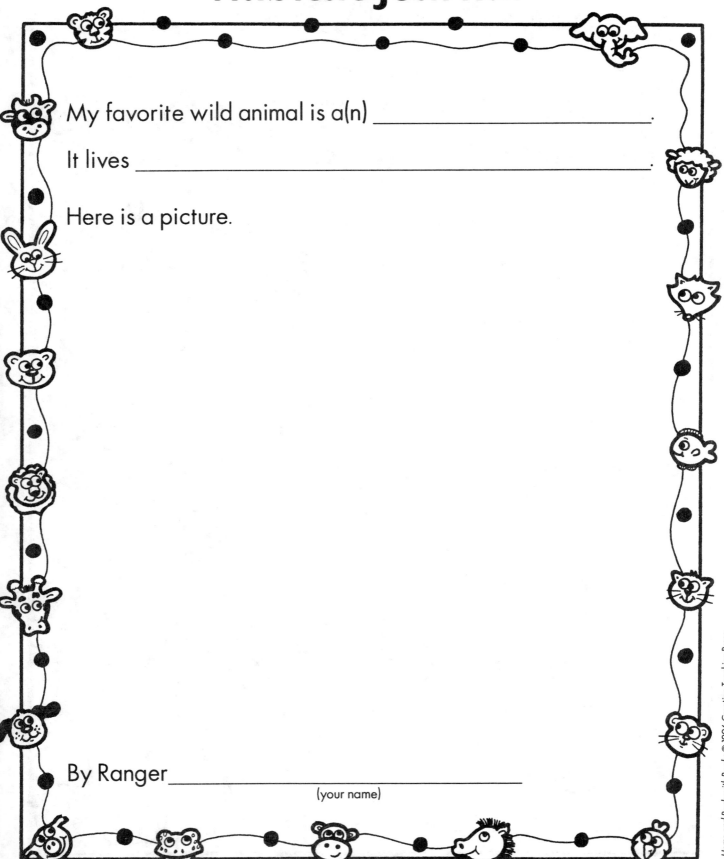

My favorite wild animal is a(n) _____.

It lives _____.

Here is a picture.

By Ranger_____
(your name)

Home and Back with Books © 1996 Creative Teaching Press

Is It Alive? Knapsack

Dear Family,

Tonight your child brought home the Is It Alive? Knapsack to share what he or she has learned about living and non-living things. Enjoy reading the enclosed story together and completing the sorting activity.

1. Read the science book.

2. Sort the pictures into groups of living and non-living things. Remember, living things take in air and nutrients (food), grow, and reproduce.

3. Discuss why you put each picture in its group.

4. Take a walk in your house, backyard, or neighborhood, observing living and non-living things with the magnifying glass.

5. On a journal page, draw a picture of one living and one non-living thing you observed on your walk.

Have fun, and please return the Is It Alive? Knapsack tomorrow for another scientist to enjoy!

Science

Is It Alive? Journal

_____ is a living thing.

_____ is a non-living thing.

By Scientist_____
(your name)

BUSINESS REPLY MAIL

FIRST-CLASS MAIL PERMIT NO. 17 CYPRESS CA

POSTAGE WILL BE PAID BY THE ADDRESSEE

TEAMWORKS CONSULTANT
CREATIVE TEACHING PRESS
P.O. BOX 6017
CYPRESS, CA 90630-9919

A Division of Creative Teaching Press

We appreciate your interest in Parent Involvement

Please take a moment to provide us with a bit of information to help us serve you better.

Name _____

Address _____

_____

Telephone Number _____ **Grade level** _____

❏ I am interested in a parent-involvement program for beginning readers.

In what other areas of parent involvement are you interested? _____

_____

Teamworks™, 10701 Holder St., Cypress, CA 90630
e-mail: **we.listen@creativeteaching.com**

Matter Box

What's Inside . . .
- *I See Colors*
- family letter (page 66)
- journal (page 67)
- small objects (toy cars, blocks, plastic foods, marbles)
- pencil/crayons

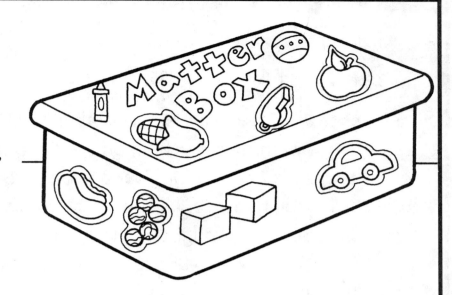

plastic box decorated with stickers of toys, cars, and food

More Take-Home Titles
Gray Rabbit's Odd One Out by Alan Baker (Kingfisher)
Sorting by Henry Pluckrose (Childrens Press)

Matter Melt Bag

What's Inside . . .
- *It's Melting!*
- family letter (page 68)
- paper cups

cloth bag with a painted dripping ice-cream cone

More Take-Home Titles
Ice Is . . . Whee! by Carol Greene (Childrens Press)
What Happened? (Creative Teaching Press)

Matter Box

Dear Family,

In science we have been learning about matter. Did you know that everything on Earth is made of matter? We can use our senses to classify matter by color, shape, texture, and function. Tonight your child brought home a book about matter to share with you. Have fun reading together, and enjoy sorting the materials in the Matter Box!

1. Read the matter book.

2. See how many different ways you can use your senses to sort the objects into groups.

3. Complete a page of the Matter Journal, drawing and writing about one way you sorted the objects. For example, by color, size, texture, or function.

Please return the Matter Box to school tomorrow for another scientist to enjoy!

Home and Back with Books © 1996 Creative Teaching Press

Matter Journal

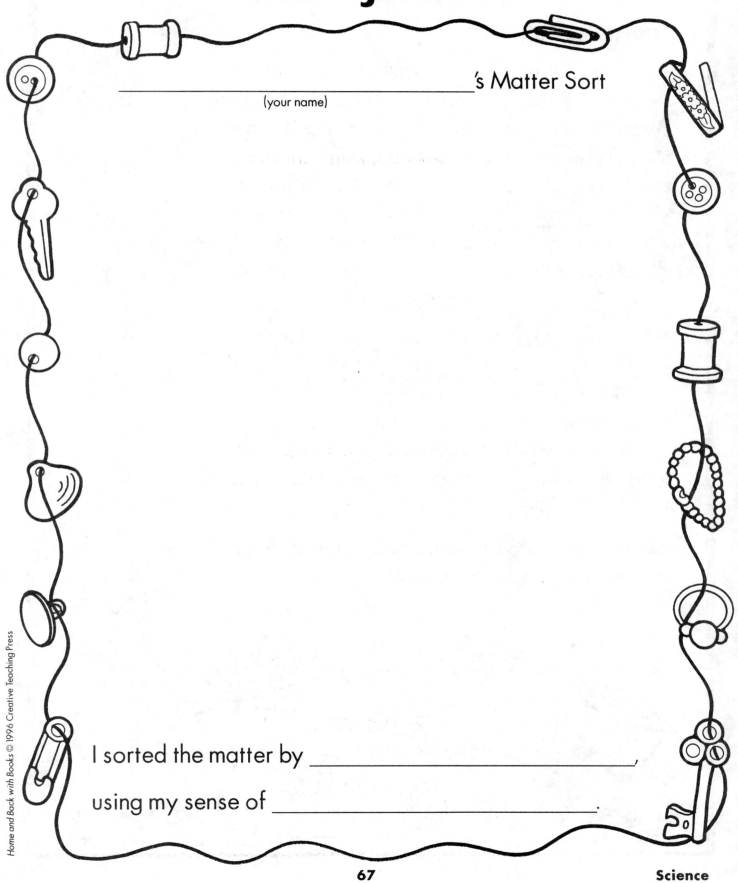

_____'s Matter Sort
(your name)

I sorted the matter by _____,

using my sense of _____.

Science

Matter Melt Bag

Dear Family,

In science we have been learning how matter can change form. Tonight your child brought home a special matter book and science experiment to share with you. Have fun reading and completing the experiment!

1. Read the matter book.

2. Discuss how items in the story change form. What can make them change?

3. Try the "Matter Meltdown Experiment":
   - Place an ice cube in each of two cups.
   - Place the cups in different areas of your home.
   - Predict which ice cube will melt first.
   - Wait for the ice cubes to melt. Were you correct? Why or why not?

Have fun experimenting, and please return the Matter Melt Bag tomorrow!

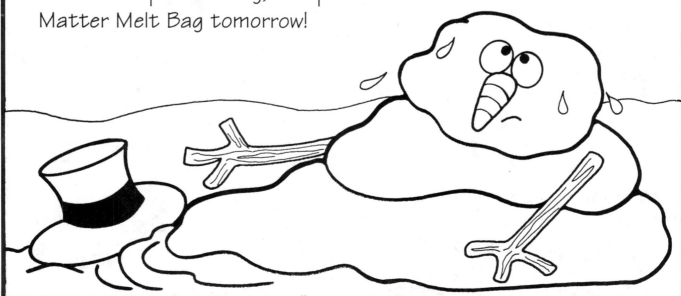

Home and Back with Books © 1996 Creative Teaching Press

Nature Knapsack

What's Inside . . .
- *If a Tree Could Talk*
- family letter (page 70)
- Nature Picture Cards (page 71)
- scissors
- crayons
- hole punch
- curling ribbon

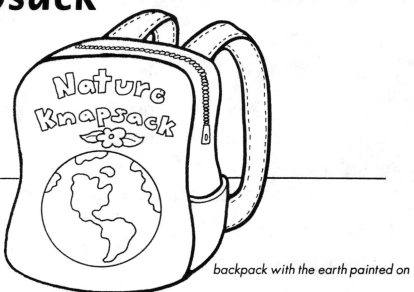

backpack with the earth painted on

More Take-Home Titles
The Great Kapok Tree by Lynn Cherry (Harcourt Brace Jovanovich)
Let's Take Care of the Earth (Creative Teaching Press)
Once There Was a Tree by Natalia Romanova (Pied Piper)

Noise Knapsack

What's Inside . . .
- *Mr. Noisy*
- family letter (page 72)
- Noise Cards (page 73)
- 6 film canisters (numbered 1–6 on bottoms), each filled with a different noise-making item (bells, beans, pebbles, rice, pennies, salt)

backpack decorated with a face surrounded by noise words

More Take-Home Titles
Noisy Nora by Rosemary Wells (Dial)
Polar Bear, Polar Bear, What Do You Hear? by Bill Martin, Jr. (Holt)
The Very Quiet Cricket by Eric Carle (Philomel)

Science

Nature Knapsack

Dear Family,

In science we have been learning about keeping our earth safe and clean for people, plants, and animals. Tonight your child brought home an earth book and activity to share with you. Enjoy reading together and making a "Nature Necklace."

1. Read the earth story.

2. Discuss the importance of keeping our earth clean and how we all do our part to help.

3. Color the nature picture cards, cut them out, and string them on ribbon to make a Nature Necklace.

Thank you for taking care of the earth, and please return the Nature Knapsack to school tomorrow!

Nature Picture Cards

Color, cut out, and string these pictures to make a Nature Necklace.

Science

Noise Knapsack

Dear Family,

We have been learning about our sense of hearing. Enjoy reading the enclosed book with your child and completing the hearing experiments!

1. Read the hearing book.

2. Shake each of the canisters and listen to the sounds they make. Don't peek inside!

3. Match the canisters to the Noise Cards. Check to see if you are correct by matching the number on the bottom of the canister to the number on the card.

Happy listening! Please return the Noise Knapsack tomorrow!

Noise Cards

Shake the canisters and guess what's inside.
Match each canister with a card.

1 bells

2 beans

3 pebbles

4 rice

5 pennies

6 salt

Science

Penguin Pack

What's Inside . . .
- *What Happened?*
- family letter (page 75)
- toy penguin

canvas tote bag with painted penguins

More Take-Home Titles
Cuddly Duddly by Jez Alborough (Viking)
Tacky the Penguin by Helen Lester (Houghton Mifflin)

Pocket Pack

What's Inside . . .
- *What's In My Pocket?*
- family letter (page 76)
- small objects easily identified by touch (key, rock, marble, toy car, cotton)
- pencil

children's denim shorts with legs sewn shut, extra pockets sewn on

More Take-Home Titles
Touch (from the *Five Senses* series) by Maria Ruiz (Barron)
My Five Senses by Aliki (HarperCollins)

Penguin Pack

Dear Family,

In science we have been learning about matter and how it changes form. Tonight your child brought home a special book and toy penguin to play with. Enjoy reading and completing the following activities together:

1. Read the book. Discuss what happened to the matter in the story and why.

2. Complete "The Antarctic Race."
   • During your bath, place two ice cubes in the water.
   • Quickly predict which ice cube will melt first.
   • Discuss what happened.
   • When you're done with your bath, reread the story to the penguin.

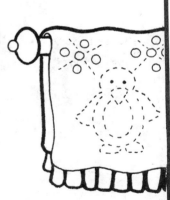

3. What are some other ways matter changes form?

Have a good time, and please return the Penguin Pack tomorrow!

Science

Pocket Pack

Dear Family,

Tonight your child brought home the Pocket Pack to share with you. We have been discussing our five senses and are working with the sense of touch. Enjoy reading the book and exploring the Pocket Pack together.

1. Read the book about the sense of touch.

2. Using only your sense of touch, reach into the pockets and guess what's inside. Don't peek! Have a family member write what you think is in each pocket. When you have reached into all the pockets, go back and check your answers.

Please put all items back in the pockets and return the pack to school tomorrow for someone else to enjoy.

Have fun!

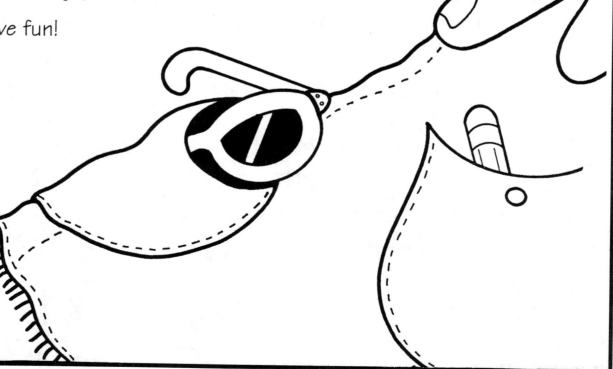

Home and Back with Books © 1996 Creative Teaching Press

Pumpkin Planting Pail

What's Inside . . .

- *The Seed Song*
- family letter (page 78)
- plastic bag of soil
- pumpkin seeds
- large, clear plastic cup
- small hand shovel

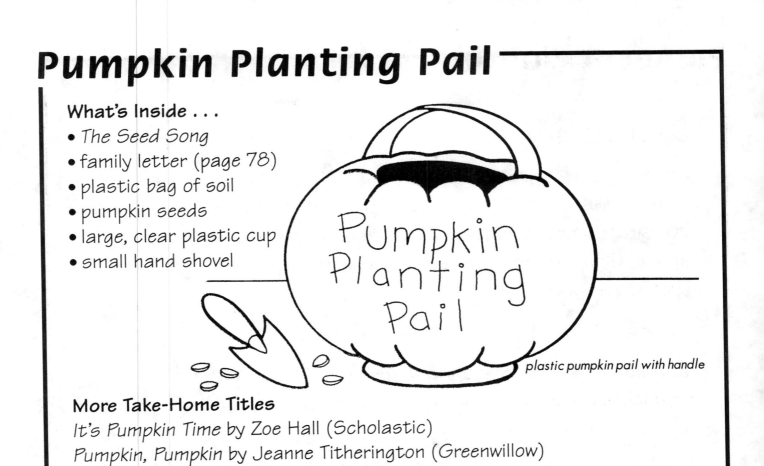

plastic pumpkin pail with handle

More Take-Home Titles

It's Pumpkin Time by Zoe Hall (Scholastic)
Pumpkin, Pumpkin by Jeanne Titherington (Greenwillow)

Recycle Bin

What's Inside . . .

- *Reduce, Reuse, Recycle*
- family letter (page 79)
- journal (page 80)
- recycled items (wrapping paper, ribbon, newspaper, foil)
- scissors
- glue
- pencil

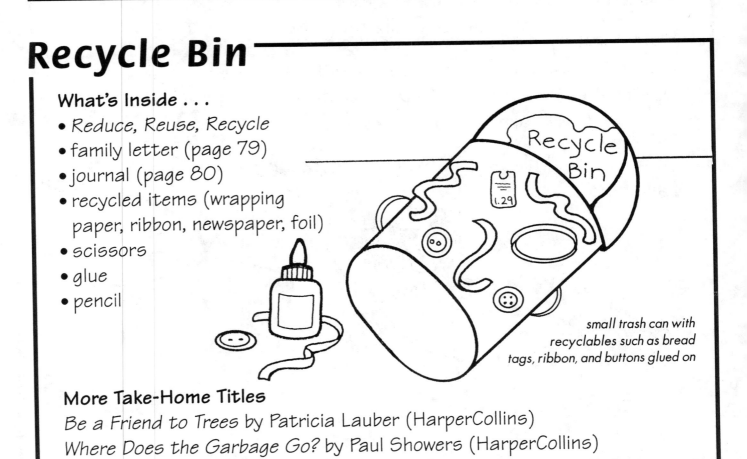

small trash can with recyclables such as bread tags, ribbon, and buttons glued on

More Take-Home Titles

Be a Friend to Trees by Patricia Lauber (HarperCollins)
Where Does the Garbage Go? by Paul Showers (HarperCollins)

Science

Pumpkin Planting Pail

Dear Family,

In science we have been discussing the special things plants need to grow. Tonight your child brought home a book and gardening activity to share with you. Enjoy reading together, and happy gardening!

1. Read the book about growing seeds.

2. Discuss the things a plant needs to grow (soil, air, water, sunlight).

3. Fill the cup with soil. Plant five seeds against the sides of the cup.

4. Set the cup on a windowsill and water when needed.

5. The plant is yours to keep! Predict how many days it will take to start growing.

Have fun, and please return the Pumpkin Planting Pail tomorrow.

Recycle Bin

Dear Family,

In science we have been learning about recycling. Tonight your child brought home the Recycling Bin containing a special book to read and activity to complete. Enjoy reading and working together!

1. Read the recycling book.

2. Discuss the recycled items in the story and why recycling is important. What items in your home can you recycle?

3. Use the recycled items to create a collage in the Recycling Journal.

4. Try to find items in your home such as bread tags, used wrapping paper, yarn, and newspaper to add to the Recycle Bin.

Thank you for keeping the earth clean! Please return the Recycle Bin tomorrow.

Science

Recycle Journal

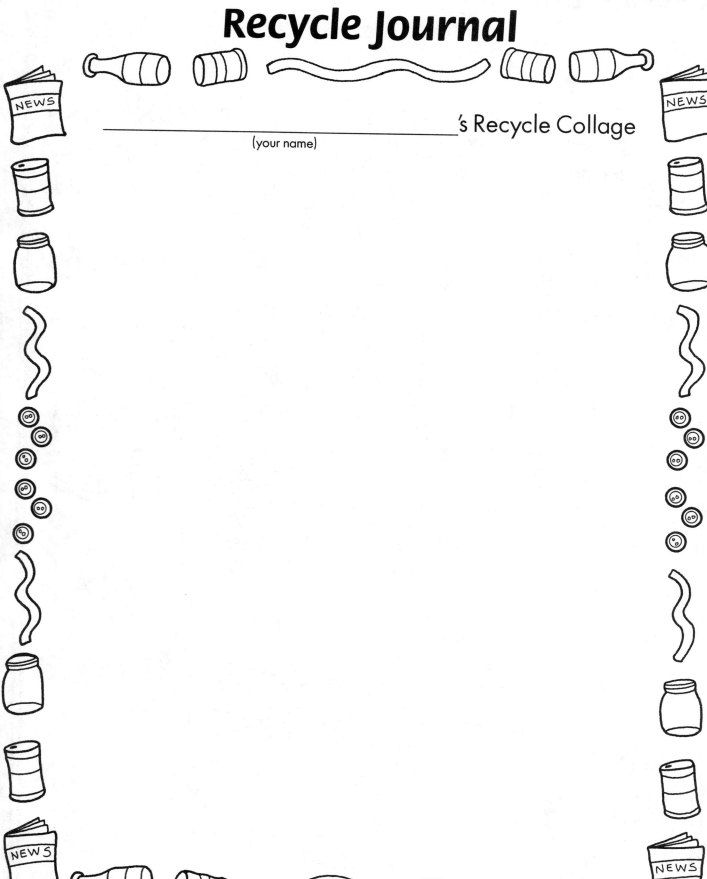

_____'s Recycle Collage

(your name)

Home and Back with Books © 1996 Creative Teaching Press

Season Sack

What's Inside . . .
- *Round and Round the Seasons Go*
- family letter (page 82)
- *Seasons Pictures* (page 83)
- scissors
- glue
- sentence strip
- stapler
- transparent tape
- crayons

canvas tote bag decorated with pictures of trees through the four seasons

More Take-Home Titles
Apple Tree! Apple Tree! by Mary Blocksma (Childrens Press)
Caps, Hats, Socks, and Mittens by Louise Borden (Scholastic)
The Four Seasons (Creative Teaching Press)

Seed Sack

What's Inside . . .
- *We Can Eat the Plants*
- family letter (page 84)
- journal (page 85)
- fruit and vegetable seeds
- paper cup
- plastic bag of soil
- pencil/crayons

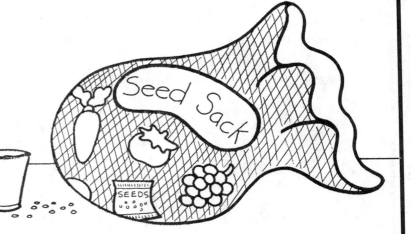

burlap bag with painted fruits, vegetables, and seed packets

More Take-Home Titles
The Carrot Seed by Ruth Krauss (HarperCollins)
Growing Vegetable Soup by Lois Ehlert (Harcourt Brace Jovanovich)
Planting a Rainbow by Lois Ehlert (Harcourt Brace Jovanovich)

Science

Season Sack

Dear Family,

In science we have been learning about the four seasons. Tonight your child brought home the Season Sack to share with you. Have fun reading the enclosed book together and making a Four Seasons Headband.

1. Read the seasons book.

2. Name the four seasons. Which is your favorite? Why?

3. Color and cut out the seasons pictures and glue them to a sentence strip. Staple or tape the sentence strip ends to make a headband.

4. Reread the story, pointing to the pictures on your headband as you read to see how it goes around just like the seasons!

Have fun, and please return the Season Sack tomorrow!

Home and Back with Books © 1996 Creative Teaching Press

Seasons Pictures

Cold, white snow,
Winds that blow,
I see winter.

Bumblebees,
Flowers and trees,
I see spring.

Warm, yellow sun,
Children having fun,
I see summer.

Orange, yellow, and brown,
Leaves falling on the ground,
I see fall.

Science

Seed Sack

Dear Family,

In science we have been learning that many plants give us food. Tonight your child brought home the Seed Sack. Have fun reading and planting seeds together!

1. Read the seed book.

2. Fill the cup with soil and choose a fruit or vegetable to grow. Plant four or five of the same kind of seed in the soil. Place the cup in a sunny area and water when necessary.

3. In the Garden Journal, draw a picture of the plant you will grow and label the parts you can eat.

Have fun gardening! Please return the Seed Sack to school tomorrow.

Garden Journal

Gardener _____ planted _____ seeds.
(your name)

Here is what the plant will look like.

Science

Senses Suitcase

What's Inside . . .
- *Where Are You Going?*
- family letter (page 87)
- journal (page 88)
- pencil/crayons

plastic suitcase with painted eyes, ears, nose, hands, and mouth

More Take-Home Titles

The Five Senses by Maria Ruiz (Barron)

Here Are My Hands by Bill Martin, Jr. and John Archambault (Holt)

My Five Senses by Aliki (HarperCollins)

Sleep Tight Sack

What's Inside . . .
- *I Can't Sleep*
- family letter (page 89)
- journal (page 90)
- teddy bear and blanket
- pencil/crayons

drawstring bag with moon and stars painted on

More Take-Home Titles

Good Night by Claire Masurel and Marie H. Henry (Chronicle)

Humphrey's Bear by Jan Wahl (Holt)

Where's My Teddy? by Jez Alborough (Candlewick)

Senses Suitcase

Dear Family,

In science we have been learning how our five senses help us experience the world. Tonight your child brought home a special book to share and activity to complete. Have fun working together!

1. Read the book about the five senses.

2. Discuss how the characters in the story use their five senses.

3. Think of a favorite place. Record the things you will experience there in the Guess Where I Am Going Journal.

Have fun, and please return the Senses Suitcase tomorrow!

Guess Where I Am Going Journal

I am going where I can see _____.

I am going where I can feel _____.

I am going where I can hear _____.

I am going where I can taste _____.

I am going where I can smell _____.

I am going to _____

Here is a picture.

By _____

(your name)

Home and Back with Books © 1996 Creative Teaching Press

Sleep Tight Sack

Dear Family,

In science we have been learning about day and night. Tonight your child brought home a special teddy bear and book to read. Enjoy sharing the book and completing the activity.

1. Read the nighttime story.

2. What special toy do you like to sleep with?

3. Complete a page of the Sleepy Time Journal and tell what toy helps you sleep better. If you do not have a nighttime friend, use Teddy in your picture.

4. Make a special place for Teddy with you tonight.

Sleep tight! Please return the sack tomorrow.

Science

Sleepy Time Journal

Bringing my _____ to bed helps me sleep better.

Here is a picture of me and my nighttime friend.

By_____

(your name)

Watch Me Grow Bag

What's Inside . . .
- *See How It Grows*
- family letter (page 92)
- journal (page 93)
- glue or tape
- tape measure
- pencil/crayons

tote bag decorated with pictures of children's faces

More Take-Home Titles
I'm Growing by Aliki (HarperCollins)
When I Was Little by Jamie Lee Curtis (HarperCollins)
You'll Soon Grow into Them, Titch by Pat Hutchins (Greenwillow)

Weather Wizard Bag

What's Inside . . .
- *What's the Weather Like Today?*
- family letter (page 94)
- journal (page 95)
- Weather Wizard Picture Cards (page 96)
- wizard's cape
- magic wand (glitter-covered wooden dowel)
- plastic thermometer
- pencil/crayons

drawstring bag decorated with weather symbols

More Take-Home Titles
How's the Weather? (Creative Teaching Press)
Thunder Cake by Patricia Polacco (Philomel)

Science

Watch Me Grow Bag

Dear Family,

In science we have been studying living things. We have learned that all living things grow and change. Enjoy sharing the special book and activity in the Watch Me Grow Bag!

1. Read the science book.

2. Discuss how the things in the story change over time.

3. Complete a page in the I Am Growing Journal.

Have fun, and please return the Watch Me Grow Bag tomorrow.

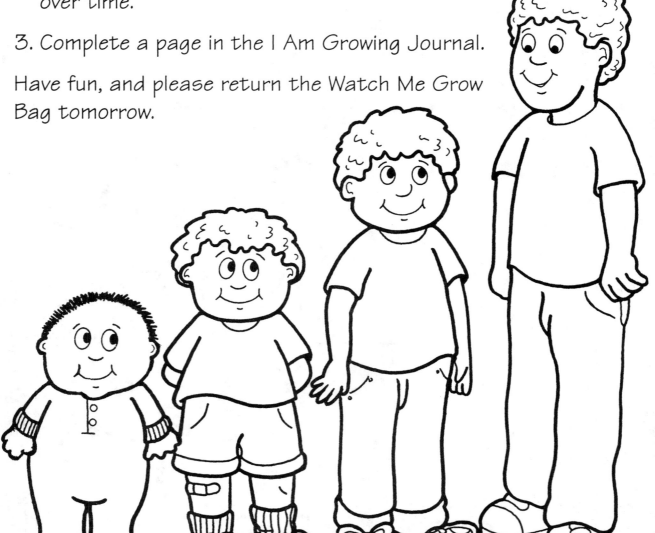

Home and Back with Books © 1996 Creative Teaching Press

I Am Growing Journal

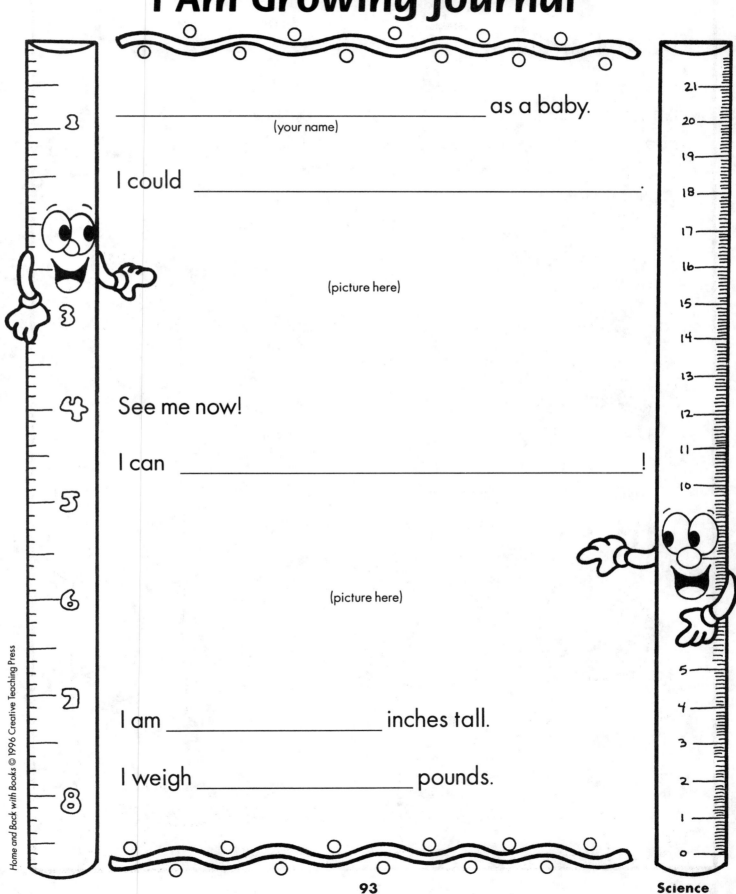

_____ as a baby.
(your name)

I could _____.

(picture here)

See me now!

I can _____!

(picture here)

I am _____ inches tall.

I weigh _____ pounds.

Home and Back with Books © 1996 Creative Teaching Press

Science

Weather Wizard Bag

Dear Family,

In science we have been learning about all kinds of weather. Tonight your child brought home the Weather Wizard Bag to share with you. Enjoy reading the enclosed book and dressing up like a "Weather Wizard" as you complete the following activities:

1. Place the thermometer outside in a safe place.

2. Put on the Weather Wizard cape and read the weather story.

3. Wave your wand, say, **Abracadabra,** and pull weather cards out of the bag, one at a time. Discuss the different types of weather. Which is your favorite? Why? Ask family members what kind of weather they like best.

4. Complete a page of the Weather Journal.

5. Bring the thermometer inside and read the temperature. Is it warm or cool outside?

Please place all items in the Weather Wizard Bag and return it to school tomorrow.

Home and Back with Books © 1996 Creative Teaching Press

Weather Journal

My favorite kind of weather is _____ because

_____

_____

_____.

Here is a picture of my favorite kind of weather.

Weather Wizard Picture Cards

Teacher Note: Color cards, cut them apart, and place them in the bag before sending the kit home.

Alphabet Soup Sack

What's Inside . . .
- *I Can Read*
- family letter (page 98)
- journal (page 99)
- capital and lowercase magnetic letters
- metal cookie sheet
- pencil/crayons

drawstring bag decorated with painted letters

More Take-Home Titles
The Alphabet Tree by Leo Lionni (Dragonfly)
Black and White Rabbit's ABC by Alan Baker (Scholastic)
Eating the Alphabet by Lois Ehlert (Harcourt Brace Jovanovich)

Birthday Backpack

What's Inside . . .
- three or more books about birthdays
- family letter (page 100)
- journal (page 101)
- birthday card and small gift
- pencil/crayons

book bag decorated with birthday designs and the words Happy Birthday

More Take-Home Titles
Birthday Presents by Cynthia Rylant (Franklin Watts)
Happy Birthday Dear Duck by Eve Bunting (Houghton Mifflin)
Mouse's Birthday by Janet Yolen (Sandcastle)
What's Going On? (Creative Teaching Press)

Alphabet Soup Sack

Dear Family,

We are working very hard learning our letter names and sounds in reading. We know that letters make words, and words are fun to read! Tonight your child brought home a special book to share with you. Please help him or her complete the following steps:

1. Read the story.

2. Using the magnetic letters on the cookie sheet, try the following activities:
   - Put the letters in ABC order.
   - Try matching capital letters to lowercase letters.
   - Name the lowercase letters.
   - See how many letter sounds you can make.
   - Spell your name and names of family members.
   - See how many other words you can spell.

3. In the Alphabet Soup Journal, write words you can read.

Have a yummy time! Please place all supplies in the sack and return it to school tomorrow.

Home and Back with Books © 1996 Creative Teaching Press

Alphabet Soup Journal

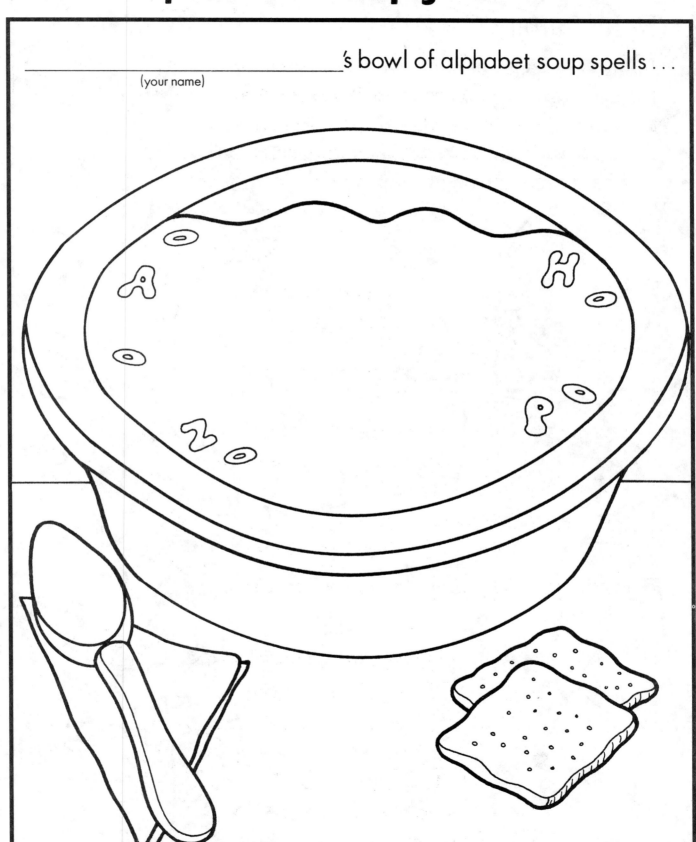

_____'s bowl of alphabet soup spells . . .

(your name)

    Just-for-Fun

Birthday Backpack

Dear Family,

Today is my special day, and I brought home the Birthday Backpack! Inside are birthday books I can read with you tonight. Then I can fill out a page in the Birthday Journal. The gift and card are for me to keep!

Home and Back with Books © 1996 Creative Teaching Press

Birthday Journal

Happy Birthday to _____!
(your name)

Today is my birthday! I am _____ years old.

To celebrate my birthday, I will

_____

_____

_____ .

Here is a picture.

Color Bear Backpack

What's Inside . . .
- *Barney Bear Gets Dressed*
- family letter (page 103)
- journal (page 104)
- Color Bear Patterns (page 105)
- small pizza box lined with felt
- pencil/crayons

backpack with a teddy bear and crayons sewn on

More Take-Home Titles
Color Dance by Ann Jonas (Greenwillow)
I See Colors (Creative Teaching Press)
Mary Wore Her Red Dress and Henry Wore His Green Sneakers
    by Merle Peek (Clarion)

Froggy Fun Pack

What's Inside . . .
- *Little Green Frog*
- family letter (page 106)
- Frog Puppet Pattern
  (page 107)
- paper lunch bag
- glue
- scissors
- crayons

tote bag decorated with painted frogs

More Take-Home Titles
Green Wilma by Tedd Arnold (Dial)
It's Mine by Leo Lionni (Knopf)
Jump Frog Jump by Robert Kalan (Mulberry)

Color Bear Backpack

Dear Family,

In school we have been learning about colors. Tonight your child brought home the Color Bear Backpack to share with you. Enjoy sharing the enclosed color story and playing with the color bear!

1. Read the color story.

2. Use the felt clothing to dress the bear in different color combinations. Name the colors each time. For example, **My bear has a red hat, blue shirt, and yellow shoes.** See how many different combinations you can make.

3. Complete one page of the Color Bear Journal by drawing a special outfit for the bear to wear.

Enjoy, and be sure to return the Color Bear Backpack tomorrow!

Just-for-Fun

Color Bear Journal

My color bear likes to wear a _____ hat, a

_____ shirt, _____ pants,

and _____ shoes.

Bear's outfit designed by _____.

(your name)

Color Bear Patterns

Teacher Note: In advance, cut several different colors of each clothing article from felt to include in the kit.

Froggy Fun Pack

Dear Family,

We have been enjoying dramatic play at school. The Froggy Fun Pack contains a book for you and your child to share and act out using a puppet. Have fun working together on the following activities:

1. Read the frog book.

2. Make your own frog puppet using the enclosed supplies. The puppet is yours to keep!

3. Reread the book using the frog puppet to act out the story.

4. Have a family member suggest ways your frog can move about (e.g., swim, skip, run, jump, and hop on one foot).

Have fun, and be sure to return the Froggy Fun Pack tomorrow!

Home and Back with Books © 1996 Creative Teaching Press

Frog Puppet Pattern

Color and cut out the pieces.
Glue them to a paper bag to make a puppet.

Just-for-Fun

Helping Handbag

What's Inside . . .
- *Who Will Help?*
- family letter (page 109)
- journal (page 110)
- pencil/crayons

backpack with painted pictures of children helping

More Take-Home Titles

The Little Red Hen by Paul Galdone (Houghton Mifflin)
The Little Yellow Chick by Joy Cowley (Wright Group)

Kitty Carrier

What's Inside . . .
- *Scaredy Cat Runs Away*
- family letter (page 111)
- journal (page 112)
- cat puppet
- pencil/crayons

small cardboard pet carrier from a pet store

More Take-Home Titles

Look Out, Patrick! by Paul Geraghty (Macmillan)
Rosie the Hen by Pat Hutchins (Scholastic)

Helping Handbag

Dear Family,

In social studies we have been learning about sharing and helping. Tonight your child brought home a special story and activity to share with you. Enjoy working together to complete the following steps:

1. Read the helping story.

2. Discuss how the characters in the story helped or did not help other characters. How could the characters have been more helpful?

3. Complete a page of the Helping Hand Journal, telling who you can help and how.

Thank you for being such a great helper! Please return the Helping Handbag tomorrow.

Just-for-Fun

Helping Hand Journal

I can help _____ by _____

_____

_____

_____.

Here is a picture of me being helpful.

By _____, a super helper!

(your name)

Kitty Carrier

Dear Family,

We have been learning about positional words such as **over, under,** and **through.** Tonight your child brought home the Kitty Carrier to share with you. Enjoy sharing the enclosed story and practicing positional words with the kitty.

1. Read the story. See how many positional words you can find.

2. Direct the kitty through your home using positional words. For example, ask it to go **through the hallway, under the chair, above the couch, over the bed, around the table, across the carpet, down the stairs,** and **into the kitchen.**

3. Complete a page of the Kitty Adventure Journal.

Have a great adventure, and please return the Kitty Carrier to school tomorrow!

Just-for-Fun

Kitty Adventure Journal

_____ and the kitty went
(your name)

_____ and _____
(positional phrase)   (positional phrase)

and got back in time for _____.

Here is a picture of the kitty's adventure.

Monster Mansion Tote

What's Inside . . .
- *Where Do Monsters Live?*
- family letter (page 114)
- journal (page 115)
- crayons

canvas tote bag decorated with colored monsters

More Take-Home Titles
Go Away, Big Green Monster by Ed Emberley (Little, Brown)
A House Is a House for Me by Mary Ann Hoberman (Puffin)
There's Something in My Attic by Mercer Mayer (Dial)

Monster Mask Kit

What's Inside . . .
- *There's a Monster in the Tree*
- family letter (page 116)
- Monster Mask Pattern (page 117)
- scissors
- glue
- crayons
- paper and fabric scraps
- tongue depressor

detergent box covered with self-adhesive paper and monster stickers

More Take-Home Titles
Go Away, Big Green Monster by Ed Emberley (Little, Brown)
One Hungry Monster by Susan Heyboer O'Keefe (Little, Brown)
There's a Nightmare in My Closet by Mercer Mayer (Dial)

Just-for-Fun

Monster Mansion Tote

Dear Family,

Tonight your child brought home the Monster Mansion Tote to share with you. Enjoy reading the enclosed story and completing the following activities:

1. Read the monster story.

2. On a page of the Monster Journal, design a monster and a place for your monster to live. Make sure your monster's home matches the way your monster looks. For example, a fuzzy monster lives in a fuzzy house, and a red monster lives in a red house. See how creative you can be!

Have a monster of a good time, and please return the Monster Mansion Tote tomorrow!

Monster Mansion Journal

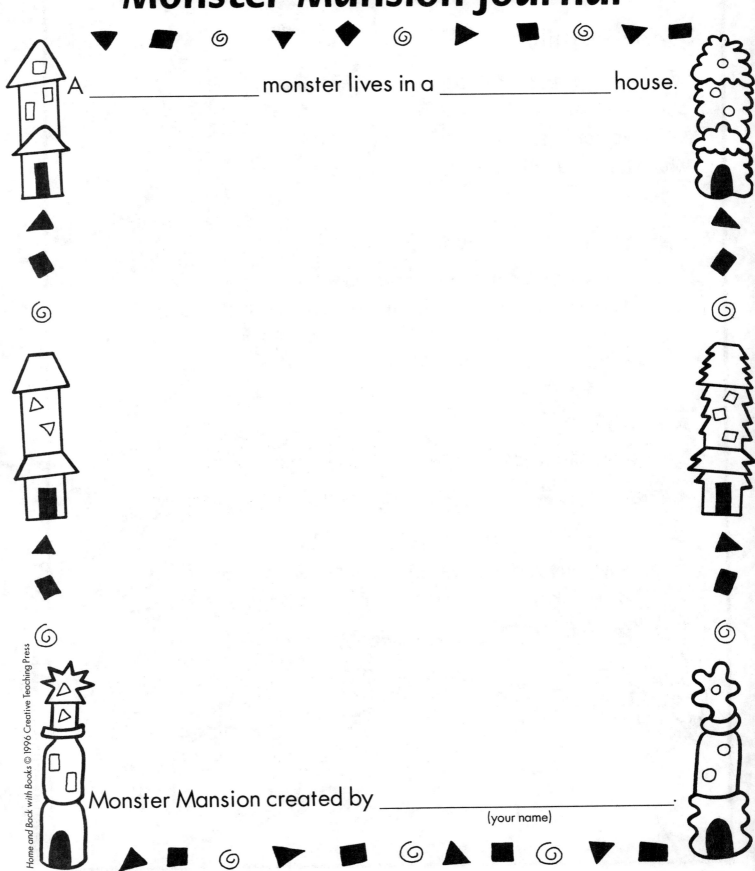

A _____ monster lives in a _____ house.

Monster Mansion created by _____.
(your name)

Just-for-Fun

Monster Mask Kit

Dear Family,

We have been reading about monsters and the funny things they do. Tonight your child brought home the Monster Mask Kit to share with you. Please help him or her complete the following activities:

1. Read the monster story together.

2. Design your own monster mask using the mask pattern and supplies. Add any other materials you have at home to make a funny monster. Use the tongue depressor as a handle for your mask.

3. Reread the book using your monster mask to act out the story.

4. Bring your monster mask to school to show the class.

If you have any fun scrap materials to add to our Monster Mask Kit, please do! Be sure to return the kit and supplies tomorrow!

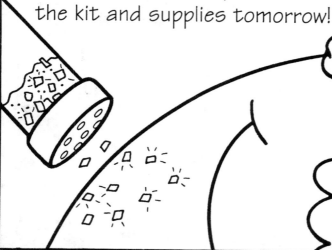
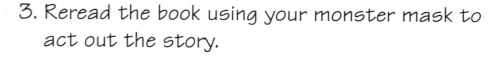
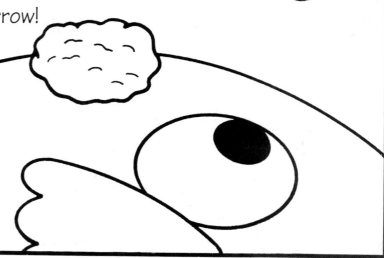

Home and Back with Books © 1996 Creative Teaching Press

Monster Mask Pattern

Just-for-Fun

Mud Pie Pack

What's Inside . . .
- *How to Make a Mudpie*
- family letter (page 119)
- Mud Pie Cookbook (page 120)
- brown play dough
- plastic work mat
- pie pan
- plastic leaves, plastic flowers, and rocks in plastic bags
- pencil/crayons

plastic tub decorated with chef's hat, pies, and kitchen tools

More Take-Home Titles
The Cake that Mack Ate by Rose Robart (Little, Brown)
Mrs. Wishy-Washy by Joy Cowley (Wright Group)
Mud by Wendy Cheyette Lewison (McKay)

Painting Pack

What's Inside . . .
- *Cat and Dog*
- family letter (page 121)
- watercolor set
- paintbrush
- painting paper
- plastic cup

plastic box decorated with self-adhesive paper and puffy paints

More Take-Home Titles
Mouse Paint by Ellen Stoll Walsh (Harcourt Brace Jovanovich)
White Rabbit's Color Book by Alan Baker (Kingfisher)

Mud Pie Pack

Dear Family,

Tonight your child brought home the Mud Pie Pack to practice reading and writing recipes. Please help your pie chef complete the following activities:

1. Read the "muddy" story.

2. Use "mud" (brown play dough), plastic flowers, plastic leaves, and rocks to make a mud pie in the pie pan. Work on the plastic mat. Add any items you would like to contribute to the Mud Pie Pack.

3. Write the recipe for your mud pie in the Mud Pie Cookbook.

Be sure to separate all rocks and flowers from the play dough and place in plastic bags! Have fun, and return the Mud Pie Pack tomorrow!

Home and Back with Books © 1996 Creative Teaching Press

Mud Pie Cookbook

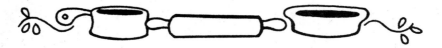

Chef _____'s Mud Pie

(your name)

1. _____

2. _____

3. _____

4. _____

5. _____

Here is a picture of my pie.

Painting Pack

Dear Family,

We have been learning about colors in school. Tonight your child brought home a color book and painting activity to share with you. Have fun completing the following activities:

1. Read the color story.

2. Cover your painting area to protect against spills. Fill the plastic cup with water for cleaning your paintbrush.

3. Use the watercolors and paper to paint a picture together.

You may keep your picture. Let paint dry overnight, and return the Painting Pack tomorrow.

Rainy Day Game Bag

What's Inside . . .
- *Rain*
- family letter (page 123)
- journal (page 124)
- games (dominoes, playing cards, simple board games)
- pencil/crayons

tote bag with silver-glitter raindrops and clouds

More Take-Home Titles
All Wet! All Wet! by James Skofield (HarperCollins)
Rain by Robert Kalan (Mulberry)
Rain, Rain, Rivers by Uri Shulevitz (Farrar, Straus)

Reading Fun Pack

What's Inside . . .
- *I Can Read*
- family letter (page 125)
- journal (page 126), 5–10 pages completed in advance
- scissors
- glue
- pencil

backpack decorated with pictures of books, signs, and ads

More Take-Home Titles
Brown Bear by Eric Carle (Holt)
I Am Special (Creative Teaching Press)
I Read Signs by Tana Hoban (Greenwillow)
I Read Symbols by Tana Hoban (Greenwillow)

Rainy Day Game Bag

Dear Family,

In science we have been discussing different types of weather and what you can do on rainy, sunny, and windy days. Tonight your child brought home a weather story and game for you to enjoy together.

1. Read the weather story.

2. Discuss things to do and ways to have fun on rainy days, such as playing games, reading, and drawing pictures. Pretend it's a rainy day, and play a game together.

3. Complete a page in the Rainy Day Journal.

Have fun! Please collect all game pieces, and return the Rainy Day Game Bag tomorrow.

Just-for-Fun

Rainy Day Journal

Rain on the _____.

Rain on the _____.

Rain on the _____.

But not on _____.
(your name)

Here is a picture.

Home and Back with Books © 1996 Creative Teaching Press

Reading Fun Pack

Dear Family,

Being able to read helps us wherever we are. Street signs, billboards, and packages are types of environmental print we read every day. Tonight your child brought home some special activities to practice reading environmental print. Please help him or her complete the following steps:

1. Have your child read the story.

2. Read the Environmental Print Journal.

3. Add to the journal by cutting out pictures from magazines, newspapers, or labels from food packages to make your own page.

Happy reading, and please return the Reading Fun Pack tomorrow!

Just-for-Fun

Environmental Print Journal

I can read _____.

ONE WAY

STOP

R R

DO NOT LITTER

EXIT

YIELD

(glue environmental print here)

By_____
(your name)

Home and Back with Books © 1996 Creative Teaching Press

Rhyming Bear Backpack

What's Inside . . .
- *Bears, Bears, Everywhere*
- family letter (page 128)
- journal (page 129)
- rubber bear stamps
- stamp pad
- pencil/crayons

bear-shaped backpack with label sewn on

More Take-Home Titles
Bears by Ruth Krauss (Scholastic)
Bears in Pairs by Niki Yektai (Macmillan)

Sequence Suitcase

What's Inside . . .
- *Under the Sky*
- family letter (page 130)
- Sequencing Cards (page 131)

plastic suitcase decorated with puffy paints

More Take-Home Titles
If You Give a Mouse a Cookie by Laura J. Numeroff (HarperCollins)
Look Out, Patrick! by Paul Geraghty (Macmillan)
Rosie's Walk by Pat Hutchins (Macmillan)

Rhyming Bear Backpack

Dear Family,

We have been learning about rhyming words in school. Tonight your child brought home the Rhyming Bear Backpack. Enjoy rhyming with the enclosed story and completing the following activities together:

1. Read the rhyming bear story.

2. Read the book a second time. Focus on what the bears are doing, and look for rhyming words.

3. Complete a page in the Rhyming Bear Journal. Use stamps to illustrate your story. Be sure your bear's action rhymes with the word **bear.** For example, **My bear is sitting on a chair.**

Have a "beary" good time! Be sure to return the backpack tomorrow for another little bear to enjoy!

Home and Back with Books © 1996 Creative Teaching Press

Rhyming Bear Journal

My bear is _____.

By _____, a "beary" good rhyme maker!
(your name)

Just-for-Fun

Sequence Suitcase

Dear Family,

We have been working on our sequencing skills at school. Tonight your child brought home a book and activity to practice sequencing. Please help him or her complete the following steps:

1. Read the story. Notice the sequence of the story. What happens first, next, and last?

2. See if you can arrange the mixed-up picture cards in the correct order. Explain your thinking.

3. Tell a story that describes what's happening in the pictures.

Happy sequencing! Please return the Sequence Suitcase tomorrow.

last

next

first

Home and Back with Books © 1996 Creative Teaching Press

Sequencing Cards

Teacher Note: Color cards, cut them apart,
and place them in the suitcase before sending home.

Just-for-Fun

Sports Sack

What's Inside . . .
- *Cinderella Dressed in Yellow*
- family letter (page 133)
- jump rope

tote bag with painted sports equipment

More Take-Home Titles
Anna Banana: One Hundred One Jump-Rope Rhymes by Joanna Cole (Morrow)

Cinder-Elly by Frances Minters (Viking)

Stamp Your Feet Action Rhymes by Sarah Hayes and Toni Goffe (Lothrop)

Tool Box

What's Inside . . .
- *Mom Can Fix Anything*
- family letter (page 134)
- journal (page 135)
- tools (scissors, hammer, nails, screws, screwdriver, tape)
- small wood blocks
- pencil/crayons

plastic toolbox with painted hammer and nails

More Take-Home Titles
Tools by Ann Morris (Lothrop)

The Toolbox by Anne Rockwell (Macmillan)

Sports Sack

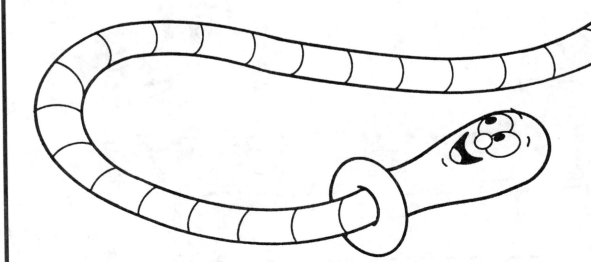

Dear Family,

Tonight your child brought home the Sports Sack to share with you. Enjoy reading and working together as you complete the following activities:

1. Read the jump-rope rhymes.

2. Practice jumping rope. Try chanting some of the verses as you jump.

3. Try jumping backwards. How many jumps can you do?

4. Lay the jump rope on the floor. Try to walk along it in a straight line.

5. With the rope still on the floor, jump from one end to the other. How many jumps does it take you?

Have fun jumping, and please return the Sport Sack tomorrow!

Tool Box

Dear Family,

We have been discussing various tools and how they help us fix things at home and school. Tonight your child brought home the Tool Box to share with you. Enjoy reading the enclosed story and "fixing" things together.

1. Read the tool book together.

2. Find a safe place to practice "fixing." Practice hammering nails into the wood block and working with the screws, screwdriver, and other tools.

3. Draw a picture of something that needs fixing in the Fix-It Journal.

Please return all tools to the Tool Box, and bring the box to school tomorrow. Any donations of nails, screws, or tape would be appreciated!

Fix-It Journal

Here is a picture of something in my house that needs fixing.

Tooth Fairy Bag

What's Inside . . .
- *Where's Your Tooth?*
- family letter (page 137)
- journal (page 138)
- pencil/crayons

canvas tote bag decorated with glitter, star stickers, and a felt tooth

More Take-Home Titles
The Tooth Fairy by Sharon Peters (Troll)
The Tooth Fairy by Audrey Wood (Child's Play)

Transportation Tote

What's Inside . . .
- *On the Go*
- family letter (page 139)
- small building blocks
- small toy vehicles (cars, buses, trucks, boats, planes)
- play map (optional)

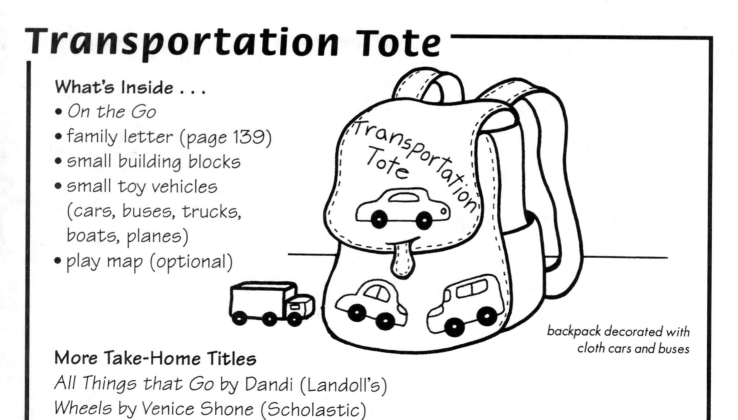

backpack decorated with cloth cars and buses

More Take-Home Titles
All Things that Go by Dandi (Landoll's)
Wheels by Venice Shone (Scholastic)
Wheels on the Bus by Maryann Kovalski (Little, Brown)

Tooth Fairy Bag

Dear Family,

Today your child lost a tooth! In honor of this special day, he or she brought home the Tooth Fairy Bag. Please help your child complete the following activities:

1. Read the tooth story.

2. Write a story in the Tooth Fairy Journal telling what you think the Tooth Fairy does with the teeth she collects.

Congratulations, and have fun!

Just-for-Fun

Tooth Fairy Journal

Dear Tooth Fairy,

I think you use my teeth to _____

_____

_____

_____ .

Here is a picture.

Love,

_____
(your name)

Transportation Tote

Dear Family,

In school we have been discussing different modes of transportation. Tonight your child brought home the Transportation Tote, including a book to share and transportation toys. Enjoy reading together and completing the following activities:

1. Read the transportation book.

2. Discuss the different modes of transportation in the story. What other modes of transportation can you name?

3. Build a city and discuss the kinds of transportation you use to get from place to place.

Have fun building, and be sure to pack up all materials and return the Transportation Tote tomorrow!

Wacky Weekday Tote

What's Inside . . .
- *All Through the Week with Cat and Dog*
- family letter (page 141)
- journal (page 142)
- Days of the Week Cards (page 143)
- pencil/crayons

canvas tote bag with days of the week painted on

More Take-Home Titles
Cookie's Week by Cindy Ward (Putnam)
Today Is Monday by Eric Carle (Philomel)

Writing Suitcase

What's Inside . . .
- *I Can Write*
- family letter (page 144)
- stationery
- envelopes
- stickers
- markers or pens

plastic box decorated with stickers of pens, pencils, crayons, and paper

More Take-Home Titles
Birthday Card, Where Are You? by Harriet Ziefert (Puffin)
The Jolly Postman by Janet and Allan Ahlberg (Little, Brown)
Leo the Late Bloomer by Robert Krauss (Simon & Schuster)

Wacky Weekday Tote

Dear Family,

We have been learning the days of the week in school. Tonight your child brought home a special book and activity to share with you. Enjoy working together as you complete the following steps:

1. Read the days of the week book.

2. Put the Days of the Week Cards in order, starting with Sunday.

3. Complete a page of the Wacky Weekday Journal by writing a funny phrase in which the objects start with the same letter. For example, **On Sunday, I eat salad wearing skates. On Monday, I eat marshmallows wearing mittens.**

Have fun, and please return the Wacky Weekday Tote tomorrow!

Just-for-Fun

Wacky Weekday Journal

 Sunday    Monday

On _____, I eat _____

wearing_____.

Here is a picture of my wacky weekday.

 Saturday

Friday

Tuesday

Wednesday

  Thursday

Days of the Week Cards

Teacher Note: Cut out cards and
place them in the kit before sending it home.

| Sunday |
| Monday |
| Tuesday |
| Wednesday |
| Thursday |
| Friday |
| Saturday |

Writing Suitcase

Dear Family,

Tonight your child brought home the Writing Suitcase to share with you. Please help him or her complete the following activities:

1. Read the story together.

2. Using the markers, pens, stationery, envelopes, and stickers, write a letter and give it to a family member or friend.

Any items you can donate to the Writing Suitcase would be appreciated. Please return the suitcase tomorrow.

Happy Writing!